111

simple ways to create
more magic every day

ADAM JAMES

YOUR F#%K YES LIFE: 111 simple ways to create more magic every day © Adam James 2023

www.yourfylife.com

The moral rights of Adam James to be identified as the author of this work have been asserted in accordance with the Copyright Act 1968.

First published in Australia 2023 by My Lifes Cool Pty Ltd

ISBN 978-0-6458485-0-2

Any opinions expressed in this work are exclusively those of the author and are not necessarily the views held or endorsed by My Lifes Cool Pty Ltd.

All rights reserved. No part of this publication may be reproduced or transmitted by any means, electronic, photocopying or otherwise, without prior written permission of the author.

Disclaimer

All the information, techniques, skills and concepts contained within this publication are of the nature of general comment only, and are not in any way recommended as individual advice. The intent is to offer a variety of information to provide a wider range of choices now and in the future, recognising that we all have widely diverse circumstances and viewpoints. Should any reader choose to make use of the information herein, this is their decision, and the author and publisher/s do not assume any responsibilities whatsoever under any conditions or circumstances. The author does not take responsibility for the business, financial, personal or other success, results or fulfilment upon the readers' decision to use this information. It is recommended that the reader obtain their own independent advice.

Dedicated to those who want to become that little bit more and squeeze the juice out of every day.

To my kids, Teisha and Hunter, who have taught me love.

To Jacqui, who always inspired me to be my best.

To those who open my heart and bring magic to me daily, I appreciate you.

A teeny amount plus some.

Introduction

It's your life. You are totally in control of the decisions you make.

Our paths are not set in stone.

Where are you headed?

This book was inspired by the many moments, learnings, readings, movies, chats, personalities, close relationships, and adventures I have been blessed to enjoy.

It's written as a quick guide to make decisions that impact the life of the person reading it.

In a nutshell, think about the simple things in life you can adjust out of your daily habits or just add to your day to make a difference.

You get to choose.

The book is intended to be a useful tool in having a ripple effect in life.

We all make a difference every day.

Consistency gets results.

If you want to be more, read the book.

If you want to create more, read the book.

If you already have an amazing life, read the book.

If you enjoy it, gift a copy to someone.

This book will make you feel that you can create change easily and in an instant.

This book is about living, not existing.

Choose one to implement, or all 111. It's up to you.

There is no formula for success, other than applying and actioning it.

Take what you need and get into living an abundant, passionate, and fulfilling F#%K YES life.

Slide sideways into your grave yelling, "What a ride!".

1

JUST ADD
The 3% RULE

If you do something 1%, 2% or 3% better than you have before, then over time, just like compounding interest, you will get a completely different result (and life).

Be committed.

[I am consistent.]

2

ADJUST Self-Doubt

Doubt or limiting beliefs show up in different ways.

Build your self-confidence muscle.

You already have all the resources inside to do or achieve anything, at any moment.

Decide and get into action. Set realistic goals. Seek support from a friend.

Adding exercise to your day can make a huge difference.

Thoughts are just thoughts, so take action.

[I am a confident person.]

3

JUST ADD
A Smile

It brightens others days and makes you feel awesome.

It's responsible for starting friendships and creating adventures.

(Give it a go, test it out, smile as you walk down the supermarket aisle... see what happens.)

[I am a great smiler.]

4

ADJUST
Judgement

Everybody is going through something. Quite often we don't have all the information and don't know what someone is dealing with, so don't assume or judge.

Adjusting judgement can be positive as it shows a willingness to be flexible, to learn, and to be adaptable.

[I am caring and kind always.]

5

JUST ADD Water

It's a key to having healthy, vibrant cells.

It helps the body absorb nutrients and remove impurities. It is the basis for life.

Give 30 ml per kilogram of your body weight per day a go.

[I am a great water drinker.]

6

ADJUST TV

Adjust the amount of TV you watch.

You can change anything or achieve new heights when you devote time to it.

Go for a walk, learn a new skill, read a book, talk to a mentor, or start a course.

Turn the TV off and get living.

[I am creating the life that I want.]

7

JUST ADD Reading & Podcasts

A little bit of knowledge can go a long way: a new perspective, some relaxing time, entertainment, creativity, or even some new ideas.

Reading and podcasts rock.

You can learn from reading. Try 10 pages a night.

Or put on a podcast while you're doing something else.

[I love reading and the gifts it provides.]

[I love listening to podcasts.]

8

ADJUST
Soft Drink

In a nutshell, it's high in sugar, artificial sweeteners and caffeine. Ultimately, you shouldn't have too much.

Try replacing it with water or juice.

[I am in charge of my choices.]

9

JUST ADD Sunshine

I don't know about you, but I love getting out in the sun for short periods of time in the mornings.

I feel better when I get my dose of vitamin D which is essential for bone health, immune function, improved mood, and overall health.

It is brilliant for the body and mind.

[I enjoy getting outdoors and into the sun.]

[I am energetic.]

10
ADJUST
(Stress)

There are many challenges in life.

One step (or bite) at a time is a strategy to manage stress.

Exercise, relaxation, meditation, a chat with a friend, or social support can all be effective tools for reducing stress levels.

[I am an action taker.]

11

JUST ADD Fun

Enjoying each moment, spending time with friends and family, playing games, and listening to music are all examples of having fun.

Finding new ways to add joy and excitement to our routines and always appreciating the little moments that bring us happiness is important.

[I like to make fun a part of everyday.]

[I am fun.]

12
ADJUST Your Silence

Stick up for yourself, your beliefs, your path, your friends, and your family.

If you don't, who will?

Don't just exist. Live today.

[I am creating my path.]

13

JUST ADD Positivity

It's your energy, nature, positive attitude, playfulness, cheerfulness, and confidence that will open opportunities and attract people in.

When you focus on the good in life, you are less likely to dwell on negative thoughts and emotions.

Being positive can have a profound impact on your physical, emotional, and mental wellbeing.

[I am a happy, healthy and fulfilled human.]

14

ADJUST
Procrastination

One of my favourite books on this topic is "Eat That Frog" by Brian Tracy.

He has two rules (tasks) for eating frogs:

1. If you have to eat two frogs, eat the ugliest one first.

2. It doesn't pay to sit and look at the frog for very long.

Take a bite and get started.

Commitment to start goes a long way. It determines results.

[I choose to get started straight away.]

[I am chasing my dreams.]

15
JUST ADD Roses

A mentor once taught me this lesson.

It's no good just winning and getting to the top of the mountain first, if you don't appreciate and be aware of the journey and view on the way up.

Stop and smell the roses.

[I am aware of my surroundings.]

16

ADJUST "I Want To" to "I Did"

Be determined, act, and proudly say, "I did."

Yes, you can have a positive attitude and a clear vision. However, unless you get started, take that first step, show commitment and consistency, you will never get there.

Plenty want it, but you must choose to do it.

[I love to be courageous and give new things a go.]

[I am on my way.]

17
JUST ADD Lemon Water

There are many benefits: it keeps you hydrated, it is rich in vitamin C, it's great for digestion, and it assists in weight loss and alkalising the blood.

Add lemon water to your overall healthy lifestyle.

It's an easy one to add.

[Taking care of my health is a priority.]

[I am changing my circumstances.]

18
ADJUST
Laziness

It's easy to sit on the couch.

It's easy to NOT sit on the couch. (It's a choice.)

Say YES to making a change.

Take responsibility.

Get up, get going, NOW.

It's always about actions, not words.

Find a way. There is always a strategy.

If you are not 100% happy with your life in this moment, it's time to give something new a go.

[Energy is everything.]

[I am taking responsibility.]

19

JUST ADD Quotes

Look them up.

Topics on love, persistence, gratitude, wisdom, choices, growth, development.

There are thousands.

[What's your favourite quote?]

[I am curious about quotes.]

20
ADJUST
Deleting Photos

Open your phone and delete 10 to 20 photos a few times a week.

Create some space for capturing new magical moments.

Bonus thought: delete emails daily.

[I am creating space for new opportunities.]

21

JUST ADD Curiosity

Being curious and learning something gives you knowledge to make better decisions.

Be curious about someone's point of view.

Be curious about your health.

Be curious about everything.

[I love being curious.]

[I am curious.]

22

ADJUST
Relationships

There are people that don't serve you.

Get rid of negative people.

Surround yourself with like-minded, great people that will make a difference.

[Meeting new people opens new doors.]

[I am open to meeting new people.]

23

JUST ADD
Ringing Friends

Time just flies. Our friends are super important. Be the one to call and say hi.

Implement this three times a week.

They know you and support you.

[I love calling my friends.]

[I am a great friend.]

24

ADJUST Self-Talk

What do you say to yourself?

I am in control.

I have got this.

This is an opportunity.

I can take the first step.

I am responsible.

I make a difference.

I am loving towards myself and others.

[I am capable. I am worthy. I am energetic.]

25

JUST ADD

Living In The Moment

Be present, say I love you, treasure the moment.

The greatest gift you can give someone is your presence.

Take time, breathe, listen, and be aware.

We can't do much about yesterday, or tomorrow either. So, focus on today and what you are doing in the present moment.

[I love being present in the moment.]

[I am present.]

26

ADJUST
Your Wake-Up Time

Most of us have heard about the 5 a.m. club.

Start with an extra 15 minutes a day and adjust as required.

More time to get things done, exercise, plan or meditate.

Take this time for yourself.

[It's amazing what I am getting done in that extra time.]

[I am alive.]

27

JUST ADD

Listening To Your Gut

A strong feeling to do or not to do something.

Intuition: tune into you.

This can be a useful tool in situations where clear solutions don't come to mind.

[My gut feeling is that I love this book, lol.]

[I am tuning in.]

28

ADJUST
Processed Foods

Cut them out, reduce the frequency, and reap the benefits.

Good food preparation doesn't take long.

Try prioritising whole foods like fruit and vegetables, grains, and proteins.

Similar with your sugar intake: adjust it.

[It's a 'sometimes food' for me.]

[I am feeling even more healthy.]

29

JUST ADD (Goals)

You need direction and something to aim for, so set some goals.

What is something you can do today to move you closer to your goals?

What area of your life would you like to adjust?

Go for it; take the first step.

Where you put your energy will ultimately take you there. Have a goal.

Advance with purpose, confidence, and effort towards your goals.

They should stretch you, guide you and challenge your very essence.

[Once I set a goal, I need to act.]

[I am an action taker.]

30
ADJUST Regrets

It's happened to us all.

Making bad decisions, not taking action, not giving it your all.

Sometimes you don't even know how close you are to your goals.

My tip is to take the lesson and use it today for growth and self- reflection.

Don't dwell. Get amongst it and move forward.

[I'll take the lesson and move on.]

[I am learning.]

31

JUST ADD (Action)

This is it. Action.

Take it, embrace it, move it.

There are always things that need doing on your way to living your dream life.

Take charge of your life. Take action.

A new outcome awaits.

By taking action, we can confront our fears and build our confidence and self-esteem.

[I am in action today.]

32

ADJUST
Your Pre-frame

A pre-frame is used to set up a positive state.

Here are some examples.

It's going to be an awesome day.

The outcome in this meeting will be exactly what we want.

How much fun will we have today?

Imagine if you learn one thing in this next two hours that will change your life.

[You will get lots from this book.]

[I am excited by the little things I am adding in and adjusting out of my life.]

33

JUST ADD
Big Thinking

Take time for big thinking.

Be bold in your dreams and goals. Use it as an energy source for your life.

Let it unlock your possibilities. Be ambitious.

You may just achieve more than you thought was possible.

[I am thinking big.]

34

ADJUST Your Fear

What's on the other side?

There may be an obstacle standing in your way, a conversation you need to have, a deal you need to broker.

Will it happen?

Take the step. Give it a go with confidence.

Step into your fears and confront them. They are usually way smaller than what you imagine.

[Let's see what happens.]

[I am willing.]

35

JUST ADD Intention

It guides our thoughts, actions, and behaviours towards the outcome we want.

Set an intention today.

Be kind.

Be bold.

Be creative.

You choose. (You must be aware.)

It will assist us in acting a certain way based on our values, beliefs, and goals.

[I am intentional.]

36

ADJUST
Time Use

Stop wasting time. Life just goes.

Jump in now and get it done.

Is what you are doing with your time taking you closer or further away from your goals or well-being?

Establishing some healthy habits will make a huge difference.

Try setting your stopwatch for 18 minutes and do a task that needs completing.

[I have ample time to get things done.]

[I am moving.]

37

JUST ADD
"You Are Awesome"

Sometimes we just need to stop and take a moment to really appreciate and treasure who we already are.

There are so many moments that we make a difference.

We have so many qualities that we have developed over time.

Breathe in and consider your amazingness in this moment.

[I am already amazing.]

38

ADJUST
Justifying/Excuses

Cause and effect.

Eliminate excuses.

You have choices. Never give up.

Excuses can prevent us from taking responsibility for our actions and can hold us back from living fully.

Our excuses can undermine our self-esteem.

In short, take ownership.

[I am making decisions and taking ownership of who I am.]

39

JUST ADD
Passion & Energy

Energy is everything.

Enthusiasm is critical.

Stand up, change your physiology, and get moving.

Your energy will be contagious.

Shift it up a notch and be an uplifting, motivated, and optimistic person.

[I am energetic and passionate in everything I do.]

40

ADJUST

Your Blame Game

A thought: you are 100% responsible for everything in your life and everything not in your life.

Decide what you want, or what you need to learn, and go.

[I am a great decision maker.]

[I make amazing choices.]

41

JUST ADD *Gratitude*

It alters your focus and reminds you what is great in your life.

Give it a go for 60 seconds.

I am grateful for....

Some suggestions:

A gratitude journal.

Express some appreciation.

Reflect on blessings for the day.

If we really look at things, how good do we have it?

[I am grateful for today.]

42

ADJUST
Victim Mindset

No more whinging or whining about your current situation, the cards you have been dealt, the parents you have, the tragedies of your past relationships, or anything else.

The ball is in your court.

You are 100% responsible now.

[I am altering my mindset daily.]

43

JUST ADD
Abundance

Abundance is everywhere.

Have you asked for it?

It's a state of mind.

There is an abundance of resources, opportunities, and blessings available always.

[I am abundant in many ways.]

44

ADJUST
Alcohol

A win can be reducing the number of days per week you drink or even the amount you drink.

Try a week without.

Moderation is good; none is best.

But like all things in life, or in this book, you get to decide.

[It's all about your choices.]

[I am making great choices.]

45

JUST ADD Consistency

The key to results is being consistent.

Exercise, business, good food, it doesn't matter. You choose and be consistent.

Watch your life change.

[I take daily action.]

[I am consistent.]

46 ADJUST
Hesitation

What are you waiting for?

Pausing is one of my favourite things to do.

It gives you the space to consider options versus missed opportunities, regrets, or lack of progress.

Decide what works for you.

[I trust the choices I make.]

[I am on my way.]

47

JUST ADD
(Conscious Breathing)

Taking deep breaths or learning about different breathing techniques can assist in calming your body and mind.

Benefits can be a reduction in stress or anxiety, an improvement in concentration, lowering of blood pressure, a boost to your immune system and promotion of relaxation.

It's simple and powerful.

[I take note of my breathing often.]

[I am applying breathing techniques.]

48

ADJUST Drama

Do you overreact?

Do you exaggerate the situation to draw attention?

Or maybe you want sympathy?

Are you seen as high maintenance?

Try developing healthy communication skills and problem-solving strategies.

[I am using my conscious breathing skills to remain calm.]

49

JUST ADD Movement

This could be substituted by exercise, dance, or fitness.

Moving your body is a must all through your life.

Movement will adjust the way you feel at any moment.

It's a critical component of living a healthy lifestyle.

Find activities you enjoy. It doesn't matter your age; incorporate them into your daily habits.

[I love to move my body.]

50

ADJUST

What you settle for

It's a personal decision.

Consider your options. Set some new goals that align with you.

Show courage.

Live, don't settle.

You don't have to settle for things as they are now.

[It's up to you.]

[I am living.]

51

JUST ADD ⟨Nature⟩

Taking a walk along a beach, hiking through a track in the mountains, having your feet on the grass, being surrounded by snow-capped mountains, feeling the freshness of a river around your body, the sounds, or the views.

Where could you go and explore?

Get into nature often.

[I incorporate time in nature as often as I can.]

[I am recharging.]

52

ADJUST

Being True To Yourself

You are only as good as your word.

Living in accordance with your values, beliefs, and priorities, and being honest with yourself about what you want, who you are and what you stand for are critical.

Setting boundaries, speaking your truth, following your dreams, honouring what you value and embracing your unique qualities are key components of being true to yourself.

How could you be truer to yourself?

Are you stuck inside jobs or relationships that you don't love?

[Be your truthful self for you.]

[I am following my path.]

53

JUST ADD

(Bravery/Courage)

Obstacles in life occur every day.

Jump over them. Find a new way.

Smash through them, continuing to strive and advance in the direction of your goals and dreams.

This is courage. This is being brave.

[I show courage today.]

54

ADJUST
Negative Situations

They occur sometimes in life.

Identify one in your life.

What can you do to change it?

What can you do to change your attitude about it?

Some tips to cope are to practice gratitude and self-care, seek support, be mindful and focus on what you can control. Then take some action.

[I have strategies to cope with negative situations.]

[I am so grateful.]

55

JUST ADD
A Word Of The Day

Give this a go.

Choose a word to focus on and be intentional.

Here are some examples.

Love.

Energy.

Dreams.

Kindness.

Playfulness.

Curiosity.

Happiness.

Laughs.

[My word for today is…….]

56

ADJUST Everyday Chemicals

There are many chemicals in our homes, in the air and in our water.

Become aware and minimise where you can.

Open your windows, try natural cleaning products, use glass instead of plastic.

I use intermittent fasting to remove impurities from my body.

Lots can be done.

[I am reducing the chemicals around my house.]

57

JUST ADD
Meditation

This can be different for all of us.

My meditation is when I run or jump in the spa.

Listening to meditations is now also a part of my daily habits.

Benefits include reducing stress, managing anxiety, changing focus, regulating emotions, and connecting with your body.

[I am meditating often.]

58

ADJUST
(Assumption)

The key is evidence or information.

Making assumptions can lead to misunderstanding or conflict.

Communicate openly and directly and find out the perspective or circumstances.

Sometimes we must.

[I am always curious.]

59

JUST ADD Self-Improvement

Constant and never-ending improvement or self-improvement.

It is my favourite strategy.

In the end, it's up to me.

If I want change, I must change.

If I want to improve, I must improve.

I have found books, podcasts and participating in sports and business to be my greatest teachings.

If you want to have more, you must become more.

[I love to learn, be an example and be my best.]

[I am improving daily.]

60

ADJUST Your Response to "No"

How many times have we heard 'NO' (in sales)?

Reframing the meaning can be a great strategy.

I haven't given the person the information he or she needed to say YES so far.

Ask for feedback or the reasons.

Continue building the relationship as the person may be a customer in the future.

[One step closer to a YES.]

[I am enjoying the NOs.]

61

JUST ADD
Kindness

Kindness is something we all like to be shown.

It has positive impacts on happiness, improves relationships and contributes to our surroundings and overall wellbeing.

It's kind to be kind.

Or, as my Uncle Bob would say, "It's nice to be nice."

Be gentle with yourself also.

[I enjoy being kind to others.]

[I am always kind.]

62

ADJUST
Distraction

The world today has endless distractions.

Turn notifications off.

Follow this rule: If it's not getting you closer to your dreams, don't watch it, don't give it energy, don't allow it in.

Distractions disrupt our focus, reduce our productivity or effectiveness, or may even increase mistakes.

There are a few strategies that help me:

Setting my timer for specific tasks.

Finding a quiet place.

Taking breaks.

Using deep breathing.

[I am aware of how many things distract me.]

63

JUST ADD Sacrifice

Sometimes you must.
Sometimes it's freeing up time.
Sometimes it's saying NO.
Sometimes it's stopping doing something.
Sometimes it's saving instead of spending.
Sometimes it's paying for advice.
Sometimes it's going without.

[I am doing whatever it takes.]

64

ADJUST
Your Definition of Balance

We are all different. Decide on what balance means to you.

I love work because it's fun and it doesn't seem like work, so my balance might seem crazy or unbalanced to someone else.

It might be work vs play, rest vs activity.

When you do the things you love doing, you somehow don't even view balance as necessary.

[Work out what balance means to you.]

[I am choosing my balance.]

65

JUST ADD

Making Yourself A Priority

Self-care is so important.

If you look after yourself, you can look after others.

Take time out, grab a massage, catch up with a friend.

Maybe just stop for five minutes and eat lunch.

Head to training, read, watch a movie.

Make yourself a priority.

[I am a priority.]

66

ADJUST Your Focus

What you focus on you feel.

Your attitude is your choice.

Know what you want. The resources you need will show up.

Focus your energy.

Take a step.

[I feel amazing; I feel healthy; I feel abundant.]

[I am focusing on my dreams.]

67

JUST ADD
Pinky Promise

You are only as good as your word.
If you say you will do something, do it.
Even to yourself.

[I am true to my word.]

68 ADJUST
Communication

Effective communication helps build trust, establishes expectations and ensures everyone is on the same page.

Use communication to resolve conflict, build better relationships, reduce delays and errors.

Communication is key.

Get better at it.

Have more conversations.

Don't stay isolated.

Improve it.

[I am becoming a better communicator,]

69

JUST ADD
Your Uniqueness

You are you and that is perfect.

Be you: add your craziness, playfulness, love, passion, and humour.

Even with your clothes.

Be unique.

[My uniqueness is a quality I love.]

[I am unique.]

70

ADJUST
Your Strategy

There is a strategy for everything.

If something is not working, change your strategy.

The strategy that has always worked may also be the thing that's holding you back.

Something to ponder.

[I am applying and changing strategies as required.]

71

JUST ADD
A Vision Board

So many of us are visual thinkers.

Create a picture of your dream life.

Use words to describe.

Feel the sensations of making it happen.

What is on yours?

If you can imagine it, you can create it.

[I focus on my vision every day.]

72

ADJUST
The Cages

Live entirely on your own terms.

Release the cages placed on you by other people's thoughts, wants or desires or expectations.

Similarly, the expectations we place on ourselves.

It's real freedom when you live on your terms.

Trust your own sense of what is right for you and set about creating the life you desire.

[I am creating my terms to live by.]

73

JUST ADD
(Awesome)

Leave behind mediocrity, live fully, have amazing experiences.

Be awesome, live awesomely, play at an awesome level.

You might call it excellence, success, or achievement.

What's your next level?

[Being awesome is fun and rewarding.]

[I am awesome.]

74

ADJUST
Travel

Is it time to broaden your horizons?

Travel is exciting.

Get away from home.

Learn new cultures.

See amazing places.

Create lifetime memories.

It's always exciting when you have something planned.

Is it time for a new adventure?

[Travelling is good for the soul.]

[I am adventurous.]

75

JUST ADD
(Love)

Breathe. Love.

Open your heart, share, let people in.

Trust in love. It's our greatest gift.

We need love to really thrive and live.

It's a daily practice.

Love is necessary for our well-being and our growth.

It makes you feel totally connected. Nothing needs to be hidden. It's honest. It's raw.

It allows you to push futher. It feels amazing. It's simply epic.

[I am so in love. I am love. I am loving.]

76

ADJUST
Sleep

Sleep is super important for health and performing at your best.

How many hours do you get?

Tip: Turn off phones and computers an hour before bed.

[I love my sleep.]

[I am getting enough sleep.]

77

JUST ADD
A Strength Session

It's not a favourite of mine (honestly).

Strength sessions are a must in overall health.

They are underrated.

If you push your body, you push your mind.

It increases metabolism and it is the only thing that will change your body shape. It grows your muscles.

[I am getting stronger by the day.]

78 ADJUST Questions

Questions are an amazing way to alter your choices.

Find someone that has what you want; ask him or her.

What would a person who is fit and lean choose to eat?

Questions play a critical role in learning, problem solving and effective communication.

You may have seen this question in this book on another page:

Is this decision taking me closer to my goals and dreams and who I want to be, or further away?

[I ask questions always.]

[I am inquisitive.]

79

JUST ADD
Possibilities

By exploring the possibilities available to us, we can make decisions based on the pros and cons of each.

More possibilities mean more options which can lead to new directions and adventures.

It's always a great time to focus on possibilities, rather than limits or obstacles.

[I love exploring new possibilities.]

[I am seeing things as opportunities.]

80

ADJUST
The Zone You Play In

Are you always playing it safe, living in what's comfortable?

Try something new. Be brave, be courageous.

Order a new dish, put up your hand, take the first step.

You will surprise yourself. Watch the growth and development that comes from this experience.

New things, new challenges, new YOU.

[I am getting outside my comfort zone as often as I can.]

81

JUST ADD
More No's

This may surprise you. Say NO to more things.

If you get asked to do something and it's not taking you closer to your dreams, say NO.

Don't get distracted.

[I say no when I choose.]

[I am in control.]

82

ADJUST
Your Grit Level

You will get more from life when you add some grit.

Maintain your standards and perseverance; add effort and interest in pursuing your goals.

An individual that shows grit tends to be focused, disciplined, consistent and persistent.

[I am grit.]

83

JUST ADD
(Flexibility)

If you are flexible, you are powerful.

Be flexible in your reactions, flexible in your day, and flexible in your attitude.

The more flexible the person, the more he or she wins.

[I am flexible.]

84

ADJUST
Perfection

Just give it a Go. Give it your all.

Get started. Don't wait until conditions are perfect.

Don't be perfect; just be you.

My tip is to get that little bit better each time.

[I give it my best always.]

[I am me.]

85

JUST ADD
(Fulfilment)

When you do something in life, does it give you a sense of satisfaction, contentment and meaning?

If YES – then it's fulfilling.

[I am fulfilled in many areas of my life.]

[I am fulfilled in many ways.]

86

ADJUST Some Old Routines

Shake things up a bit.

The success systems that have gotten you here today may be the greatest thing holding you back.

Pivot, jump over, and blow up those old routines.

They may be an invisible obstacle.

[I am willing to give new things a go.]

87

JUST ADD
Fruits and Vegetables

Energy is everything.
Choose alkaline-based foods.
Eat some raw foods.
It's the nutrients that are the key.
What preventative strategy do you use?
Create good habits daily.

[I choose whole foods.]

[I am full of energy.]

88

ADJUST Your Zags

These may be your sneaky treats.

Or your "I just can't say no to."

Make small, smart choices or adjustments and watch the compounding benefits.

Something to consider: add a penalty that you would rather not do.

E.g., Eat an apple crumble and do 100 burpees.

[I am aware of my zags.]

89

JUST ADD Words of Encouragement

Make a difference in someone's day.

A friend, your partner, or your kids.

Give encouragement freely and make an impact.

Keep going. Move forward.

You are capable.

Believe in yourself.

Stay positive and focused.

Keep striving for excellence. Never settle.

[I believe in myself and my abilities.]

90

ADJUST
(Stuff)

Stuff, possessions, things, toys, books, glasses, clothes: they all accumulate over time.

Clear stuff out.

Let some things go and give yourself some space for the new.

[I create space for the new.]

91

JUST ADD Adventure

There are many adventure-type activities that challenge you and push you out of your comfort zone.

What is one that you have done?

What is one that you would like to do?

When will you do it?

Have you hiked, camped, mountain biked, skydived, bungee jumped, been on safari or to a festival or done rafting, sailing, or fishing?

[An adventure is waiting to be had.]

[I am excited.]

92

ADJUST
Your Start Date

Today is the best day to get started.

Don't wait until your birthday, or next Monday, or especially not the new year.

Start small or start big. Just start today.

Choose a page in this book and get started.

[I choose to start now.]

[I am not waiting.]

93

JUST ADD
Rest

An afternoon sneaky lie down, a 15-minute power nap, sitting outside for a moment: we all need rest.

Maybe it is having your feet or back rubbed.

Take 10, relax, chill, and feel the moment.

Rest, to recover and rejuvenate, is essential to function at our best.

Prioritise it for overall well-being.

[I take rests when I feel I need to.]

[I am listening to my body.]

94

ADJUST
Your Investment

You get to choose.

Invest in yourself, invest your time, invest your effort, and invest your money.

[I am investing in me and others.]

95

JUST ADD
(Accountability)

Grab a mate, your partner, ask for accountability.

Tell your partner your goal. Be bold: he or she may even do it with you.

I train better when I train with others. It is how I remain accountable.

Just knowing you are being held accountable can be motivating. It provides support and encouragement and often creates deadlines to work towards.

To stay on track, get an accountability partner.

[I like to keep myself accountable.]

[I am accountable.]

96

ADJUST
Your Course Correction

When obstacles come up, change your course, still with your goal in mind.

There is always a way.

Don't settle.

Looking at where you are at and making the correction may be the path you need to take.

Remember: you are only defeated if you stop.

It's an adjustment.

Analyse, then focus on a solution.

[I am flexible and change my course if needed.]

97

JUST ADD M.A.D. / Contribution

Making a difference in others' lives is such a joyful experience.

Buy a stranger a coffee; pay for someone's fuel.

Be passionate about giving.

Contributing to others is so good for the soul.

[I am M.A.D.]

98

ADJUST Your Level of Momentum

Once you start, keep going.

Increase your output. Get a helping hand.

Do the next step.

Create your momentum.

It is a powerful force to make progress.

[Small wins turn into bigger wins with momentum.]

[I am building momentum.]

99

JUST ADD
Planning

Planning makes a difference and saves you time.

It gives clarity, focus, efficiency, accountability, and flexibility.

It is a key component to being successful.

It's your roadmap.

It lets you know where you are at.

[I plan what I want to achieve.]

[I am a planner.]

100

ADJUST
How You Show Up

You must set standards for your own success.

Be present.

Be engaged.

Listen actively.

Be respectful.

Be prepared.

Be you.

[I am present.]

101

JUST ADD
A Mentor

Choose a role model, ask questions, and imitate as closely as you can.

The person you choose doesn't even have to know you exist.

It's an invaluable tool.

A mentor provides guidance, support, a larger network, and feedback and often saves you time and resources.

[A mentor's time is valuable.]

[So is a mentor's knowledge.]

[I am super grateful.]

102

ADJUST
Your Habits

An easy way to make a difference is to stack your habits.

Somewhere. Start with one, add another, then another.

It starts with a choice. That choice may become a habit. These habits will impact your life.

Be relentless.

Long term results guaranteed.

[Habits are the ultimate.]

[I am super grateful.]

103

JUST ADD
A Green Drink

Grab your blender, some greens, vegetables, and fruits.

It is a quick and easy way to add nutrients, vitamins, minerals, and antioxidants to your diet.

There are lots of benefits: energy, mental clarity and overall cellular health, alkalising your body.

[I commit to having a green drink.]

[I am creating healthy cells.]

104

ADJUST Your Debt

Pay off debt as quickly as you can.

Find a way: an extra shift, a side hustle, a % of money weekly that eliminates debt.

[I am reducing debt.]

105

JUST ADD
Uncertainty

It's where the magic happens.

Growth and new learnings.

[I am embracing uncertainty.]

106

ADJUST
The Route You Take

Life is an incredible adventure.

Take a different route or path on your way to work.

Notice the greatness in variety.

Go on, I dare you.

[I am choosing to go different ways often.]

107

JUST ADD
A Massage

OMG, the body and mind are always grateful.

Releasing tension in your muscles, alleviating pain or stiffness, improving circulation, and boosting the immune system and your range of motion are all benefits.

Book yours today.

[YES please.]

[I am booking one today.]

108 ADJUST
Coffee

Coffee can be like a see-saw. Good and bad.

Alertness vs. Restlessness.

Increase Metabolism vs. Experience Digestive Issues.

Antioxidants vs. Addiction.

Be mindful always.

[Small, medium, large, jumbo or none.]

[I am mindful.]

109

JUST ADD Adaptogens

A group of herbs that are believed to help the body adapt to stress and promote overall health.

Look them up.

[Benefits plus.]

[I am looking after me.]

110

ADJUST
Needing Approval

It's your life.

Give things a go.

Consult with others but make decisions for yourself.

Feedback, advice, and permission are sometimes needed.

Make a judgement and go.

[I am a great decision maker.]

111

JUST ADD
A New Contact

Build your network of both personal and professional friends by reaching out, supporting, and adding value.

[I am adding a new contact a day.]

Life is open to endless opportunities and possibilities.

Be you. Choose to create the magic every day.

Love Truly Madly Deeply.

Be open.

I hope that one of these 111 has made an impact on you in some way.

That one line, thought, or decision you make takes you on a magical journey towards living a F#%K YES life.

Heartfelt thanks to my two best mates, Wade (RIP) and Bob, for such mighty friendships.

My deepest gratitude to my kids for choosing me.

To Emily Gowor for guiding me through this process.

To all my friends and family for adding to this adventure called life.

To all that have made an impact on me and caused a ripple effect.

To the many that show fight, spirit, courage, and vulnerability to be themselves.

To the one who brings me peace, love, and magic.

Ads, just one of the lads. He is a little crazy.

He loves reading, sports, self-development, and business.

He is a dad of two and lives on the Sunshine Coast, Queensland, Australia.

He loves to make an impact on anyone he meets, through being present and taking an interest in that person. He feels he can learn from everyone he meets.

He has a degree in business, is qualified as a coach, drives an Uber and has a successful online business.

What he loves the most is having fun in everything he does.

Thanks, heaps, for purchasing a copy of the book.

www.yourfylife.com

You can email Ads at chat@yfyl.com.au

My 6 Favourite Books

The 4-Hour Work Week (Timothy Ferriss)

Atomic Habits (James Clear)

The 5 Second Rule (Mel Robbins)

The Obstacle is the Way (Ryan Holiday)

Way of the Peaceful Warrior (Dan Millman)

The Way of the Superior Man (David Deida)

www.ingramcontent.com/pod-product-compliance
Lightning Source LLC
Chambersburg PA
CBHW051536010526
44107CB00064B/2741